What is TIME?

Claire Llewellyn

OXFORD
UNIVERSITY PRESS

OXFORD
UNIVERSITY PRESS

is a department of the University of Oxford.
It furthers the University's objective of excellence in research, scholarship,
and education by publishing worldwide in

Oxford   New York

Auckland   Cape Town   Dar es Salaam   Hong Kong   Karachi
Kuala Lumpur   Madrid   Melbourne   Mexico City   Nairobi
New Delhi   Shanghai   Taipei   Toronto

With offices in

Argentina   Austria   Brazil   Chile   Czech Republic   France   Greece
Guatemala   Hungary   Italy   Japan   Poland   Portugal   Singapore
South Korea   Switzerland   Thailand   Turkey   Ukraine   Vietnam

Oxford is a registered trade mark of Oxford University Press
in the UK and in certain other countries

British Library Cataloguing in Publication Data

Data available

ISBN: 978-0-19-846114-2

3 5 7 9 10 8 6 4

Printed in China

Paper used in the production of this book is a natural,
recyclable product made from wood grown in sustainable forests.
The manufacturing process conforms to the environmental
regulations of the country of origin

Acknowledgements

The publisher would like to thank the following for permission to reproduce photographs:
p4 Steve Mansfield-Devine/Alamy; **p5**l&r Katrina Lonergan/Fotolibra; **p6** Douglas Pulsipher/Alamy;
p10 Travelshots.com/Alamy; **p12**cl Photo Network/Alamy, **p12**cr Sue Colvil/iStockphoto, **p12**t Oxford
University Press, **p12**b Martin Carlsson/iStockphoto; **p14**t Pavel Filatov/Alamy, **p14**b Konrad Wothe/
Minden Pictures/Frank Lane Picture Agency; **p15**t Peter Johnson/Corbis UK Ltd., **p15**b Kennan Ward/
Corbis UK Ltd.; **p16** Mark Newman/Frank Lane Picture Agency; **p18** David Parker/Science Photo Library;
p19 Popperfoto/Alamy; **p20** Bettmann/Corbis UK Ltd.; **p22** Ronald Grant Archive

Cover photograph: Corbis/George B Diebold

Illustrations by Bill Bolton/Advocate: **p4**, **p5**, **p20**, **p21**, **p22**, **p23**;
Julian Baker: **p6**t, **p7**, **p8/9**, **p11**, **p13**, **p16**, **p17**, **p18**

CONTENTS

WHAT IS TIME?

What time do you have to get up in the morning? When does school start? What time do you go to bed at night? Time sometimes seems to rule our lives. We often find ourselves looking at the clock; we always want to be 'on time'.

Time is a bit of a mystery. We can't see it, but we notice changes as it passes by. Every day our hair grows longer: we say that it's 'no time' until it needs cutting again. Family and school photos show how much we change in a single year!

Clocks measure time, of course, but we all have our own way of *feeling* time pass. A film might last 90 minutes but people will feel the time differently. If the film bores you, the time seems endless; if you're hooked, it flashes by.

This book is all about 'time'. It discusses how we measure time, how it affects living things, and how it can behave in surprising ways. The book also includes lots of sayings – a record of our fascination with the subject of 'time'.

"What is Time? If no one asks me, I know. But if I wanted to explain it to one who asks me, I plainly do not know."
St Augustine (354–430), a Christian thinker

TIMEKEEPER EARTH

Did you know that the way we measure time is based on the movement of our planet? Our year is based on the time it takes for the Earth to **orbit** the Sun.

As the Earth orbits the Sun, it also spins on its own **axis**. Our day is based on the time it takes for the Earth to spin round once. It spins round just over 365 times in the time it takes to orbit the Sun. That's why we have 365 days in a year.

As the Earth spins around, half of it has light from the sun. The other half has night.

Each day is divided into smaller units of 24 hours. Each hour is divided into 60 minutes and each minute into 60 seconds. These are not natural divisions. They were fixed by the Ancient Egyptians, Babylonians and Sumerians – people who lived in the Middle East about 5,000 years ago.

Time in the Solar System

Days and years vary from planet to planet. A day depends on the speed at which a planet spins round once. On Mercury, for example, a day is very long – as long as 59 days on Earth. A year depends on the time it takes for a planet to orbit the Sun. On Mercury, a year is short – only 88 Earth days from start to finish.

Key to Diagram

1. Mercury
2. Venus
3. Earth
4. Mars
5. Jupiter
6. Saturn
7. Uranus
8. Neptune
9. Pluto

Planet	Time* taken to spin once	Time* taken to orbit the Sun
Earth	1 day	365 days 6 hours
Mercury	59 days	88 days
Venus	243 days	225 days
Mars	24 hours 37 minutes	1 year 322 days
Jupiter	9 hours 55 minutes	11 years 313 days
Saturn	10 hours 40 minutes	29 years 146 days
Uranus	17 hours 14 minutes	84 years
Neptune	16 hours 7 minutes	164 years 288 days
Pluto**	6 days 9 hours	248 years

*Time given in Earth days

**In 2006 Pluto was renamed a 'dwarf planet' There are two other dwarf planets, Ceres and Eris.

"Nae man can tether time or tide."
("No one can stop time or tide.")
Robert Burns (1759–96), a Scottish poet

KEEPING TIME

Water clock

People have always looked for ways of finding, keeping and measuring time. The earliest way of finding the time was by using shadows, which fall in different places at different times of day. The first timekeepers, such as water clocks, kept track of time indoors or when shadows could not be used. Later, candle clocks and sandglasses were invented: these were timers that measured an hour or other **intervals** of time.

Candle clock

Sundial

> "I am a sundial.
> I make a botch
> Of a thing that can be done
> So much better by a watch."
> *Ogden Nash (1902–71), an American poet*

A timeline of clocks

*c. 2000 Shadow clocks and sundials are used in Ancient Egypt.

c. 1400 The water clock: water drips out of a container.

1290 The first mechanical clocks rang a bell on the hour.

1300s The sandglass was invented.

BC

AD

*c. stands for *circa* (about)

It was only with the invention of the **pendulum** that clocks kept accurate time. All clocks work by counting. They count the swing of a pendulum or, as in most modern clocks, the **vibration** of a tiny piece of **quartz**. Atomic clocks count vibrating **atoms** in caesium, a soft, silvery kind of metal. They are the world's most accurate clocks, losing or gaining just one second every 1.6 million (1,600,000) years!

Pendulum clock

Sandglass

Atomic clock

1657 The first pendulum clock was made.

Late 1800s Wristwatches were invented.

1955 The first accurate atomic clock was made.

Local time

We all know that the Sun rises in the east and sets in the west. However, the further west you are, the later the Sun rises and the later it sets. This means that when a sundial in London says 12 noon, a sundial to the west in Plymouth, for example, will only say 11.44. This is known as 'local time'.

Standard time

About 200 years ago, all clocks were set to local time. However, the invention of railways and timetables meant that everyone needed to use the 'same' time. So in 1880 the British government decided that the local time of Greenwich, London, should become *standard* UK time.

This line at Royal Greenwich Observatory is called the prime meridian. It marks the position of 0 degrees **longitude**. All lines of longitude on the surface of the Earth are measured from this point.

		AW MX	AW	AW ◇	AW ◇ ⊞	AW ◇	AW ◇	AW	◇ ⊞
rdaugleddau / lford Haven	d								
aerfyrddin / Carmarthen	d						0500		
ertawe / Swansea 7	d			0400b		0436	0545	0600	
astell-nedd / Neath	d			0410b			0556	0610	
rt Talbot Parkway	d			0419b			0603	0619	0
en-y-Bont / Bridgend	d			0430b			0616	0630	07
aerdydd Canolog / ardiff Central	d	0020		0400	0510	0535		0650	0720	0750
ndon Paddington	d									0527
ristol Temple Meads	d						0554	0654	0715
asnewydd / Newport	d	0039		0418	0529	0550		0704	0734	0804
wmbran	d	0050		0428	0539	0558		0715	0744	0815
ontypwl / ontypool & New Inn	d	0056		0434	0545	0603			0749	
Fenni / Abergavenny 7	d	0107		0445	0555	0611		0728	0800	0828
ereford	d	0135a		0523	0625	0648		0756	0828	0856
ominster	d			0536	0638	0702		0809		0909
dlow	d			0547	0649	0713		0820	0849	0920
aven Arms	d			0556	0658	0721	0753	0829		0929
urch Stretton	d			0608	0707	0730	0806	0838		0938
rewsbury	a			0622	0722	0744	0821	0852	0915	0952
berystwyth	a				0922				1122	
rewsbury	d	0603	0626	0730	0746		0826	0854	0930	095
recsam Cyffredinol / rexham General	a			0806		0904			1006	1
orton	d		0613x	0638			0836x			
em	d		0619	0638		0758	0842			
ees	d		0623x				0846x			
hitchurch	d		0631	0647		0807	0854			
bury	d		0637x				0900x			
ch	d		0644	0656		0816	0907			
	a		0654	0705		0825	0917	0		
	a			0759	0828	0926	0927	0957		
	a			0919	0926	1024				
	a				0943	1046				

Cardiff - Shrewsbury - Crewe - Manchester
dau - Caerdydd - Amwythig - Crewe - Manceinion Dydo

International time zones

To organize timekeeping around the globe, the lines of longitude were used. These divide the Earth into 24 'slices'.

Sailors used them to measure how far east or west they were. Each 'slice' became a different **time zone** – one for each hour of the day. The UK fits inside one time zone, while the USA – a much larger country – stretches across four different zones.

0° longitude passes through Greenwich

The world's countries fit into 24 time zones, created by the lines of longitude. When you travel **west** you put your watch back for every time zone you cross. When you travel **east** you put your watch forward an hour for every time zone you cross

Chicago
London
Tokyo

-11 -10 -9 -8 -7 -6 -5 -4 -3 -2 -1 0 +1 +2 +3 +4 +5 +6 +7 +8 +9 +10 +11 +
←West **Time** East →

Chicago
6:00 a.m.

London
12:00

Tokyo
9:00 p.m.

"Remember that time is money."
Benjamin Franklin (1706–90), an American politician, inventor and scientist

TIME AND THE SEASONS

In some parts of the world the passing year brings four different seasons: spring, summer, autumn and winter. In summer the days are long and warm; in winter they are short and cold. What causes these changes?

"If Winter comes, can Spring be far behind?"
Percy Bysshe Shelley (1792–1822),
English poet

As the Earth travels around the Sun, it is tilted on its axis. On one side of its orbit, the North Pole points towards the Sun. When this happens, the northern **hemisphere** – that is, Europe and the northern parts of Asia and North America – enjoys long, light days and warmer weather.

A few months later, the Earth is on the other side of its orbit. Now the South Pole is pointing towards the Sun, and the southern hemisphere – that is, Australia, New Zealand and southern South America – enjoys its turn to face the Sun. Meanwhile, people in the north are shivering in the cold.

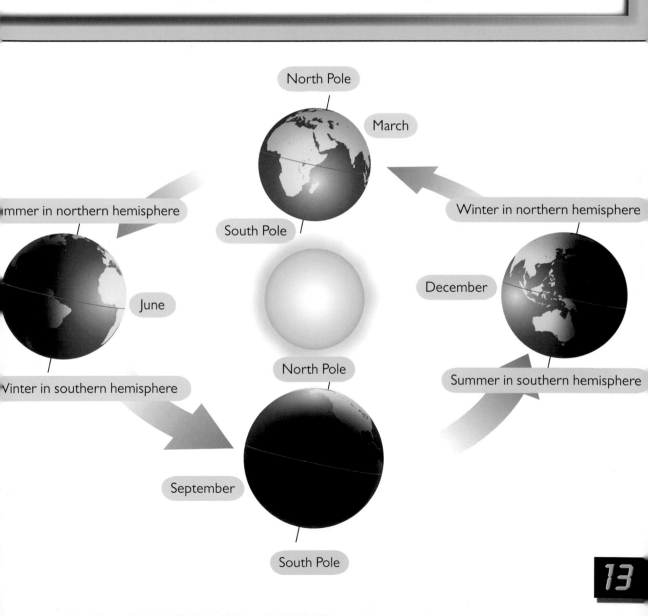

TIME IN NATURE

A change in the season

Plants and animals are aware of time and the passing seasons. Many plants flower in the spring, when conditions are good for developing seeds. But how do plants know when it is spring? Scientists have discovered that many **species** (groups of related plants), particularly those that grow on mountains, need to experience weeks of cold before they can begin to flower. This prevents them from flowering in autumn.

> "To every thing there is a season, and a time to every purpose under heaven."
> **Bible**: Ecclesiastes ch. 3, v. 1

A change in the light

Animals are sensitive to the number of hours of light in a day. Most birds breed when the days grow longer because there will be food to feed their young.

Migration

Migration means moving from one place to another, in line with the change of seasons. For example, Arctic terns fly from their breeding grounds in the Arctic south to Antarctica and then back again – all in one year. This is a distance of over 21,750 miles (35,000 kilometres)!

All change!

Some animals change their coat, migrate or hibernate as the days grow shorter. They know bad weather is on the way. Of course, such timings are not exact.

The snowshoe hare, which lives in the Arctic, depends on camouflage to hide from its predators. Twice a year, its coat changes to match its surroundings: in summer it is rusty brown; in winter it is snow-white. The change is triggered by the change in day length, so the poor hare is very **conspicuous** if snow arrives late or lasts longer than usual!

Hibernation

Hibernation means sleeping through the winter. Animals hibernate to conserve energy at a time when food is scarce. The activity in their bodies slows down and their body temperature falls.

15

GEOLOGICAL TIME

Our planet has a history of about 4,600 million years. Scientists have divided this long period of time into smaller chunks called eras. The eras mark important changes in the history of life on Earth. The evidence for this is found in fossils, the remains of extinct plants and animals that are buried inside rocks.

Precambrian Era:
4,500–540 million years – the time before most life began

Palaeozoic Era:
540–250 million years ago – the time when the first animals and plants appeared

Mesozoic Era:
250–65 million years ago – the time of the dinosaurs

Cenozoic Era:
65 million years ago to today – the time when human history began

This fossilised fish is 25 million years old.

The clock of life

It is hard for us to grasp long periods of time. To make things easier to understand, scientists have used a clock face to show how short human history is compared to the history of the Earth as a whole.

Earth's history as a 12 hour clock

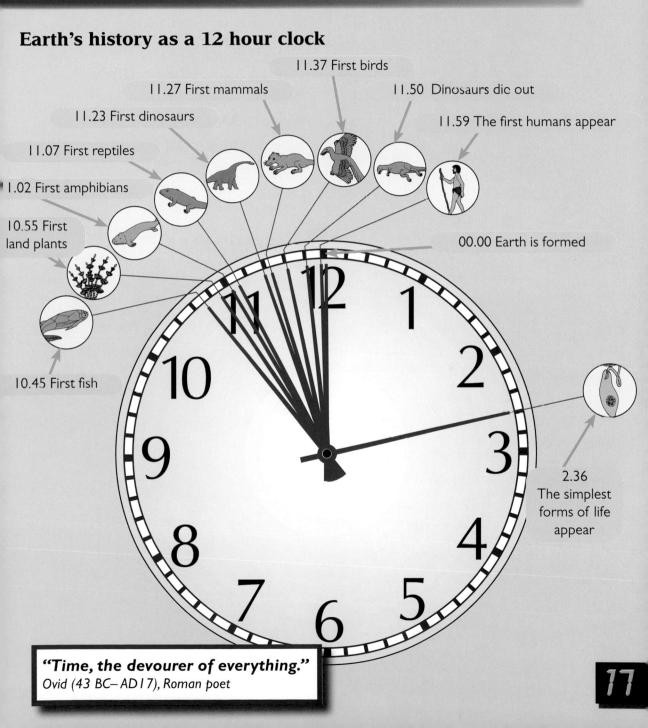

11.37 First birds

11.27 First mammals

11.50 Dinosaurs die out

11.23 First dinosaurs

11.59 The first humans appear

11.07 First reptiles

11.02 First amphibians

10.55 First land plants

00.00 Earth is formed

10.45 First fish

2.36 The simplest forms of life appear

"Time, the devourer of everything."
Ovid (43 BC– AD17), Roman poet

TIME AND SPEED

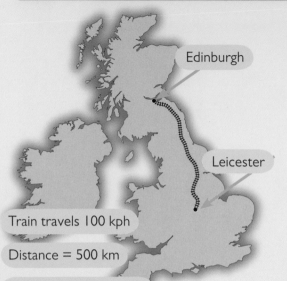

Edinburgh

Leicester

Train travels 100 kph

Distance = 500 km

Journey time = 5 hours

We use time to calculate how fast things move. If a train travels 100 kilometres in one hour, we say that it is travelling at 100 kilometres *per hour* (kph). We can then work out how far it will travel in, say, five hours.

An astronomer using a telescope at an observatory in San Francisco, USA

Calculating distance, speed and time is useful when we are travelling but it can also answer exciting questions like how big is our **galaxy**, the Milky Way?

The speed of light

The distances between the stars are so big that it doesn't make sense to measure them in kilometres, just as it wouldn't make sense to measure the distance from, say, London to New York in millimetres. Instead, astronomers use a distance based on the speed of light.

A beam of light races through space at over 300,000 kilometres per second! In a year, it travels about 9,500 billion kilometres – a distance called a light year. A light year is a measurement of distance, not of time. For example, scientists estimate that the Milky Way is about 100,000 light years across: that is 100,000 x 9,500 billion kilometres – a truly staggering size!

The Milky Way

Approximately 9,500,000,000,000,000,00 km or 100,000 light years

"Space is big. Really big. You just won't believe how hugely, mind bogglingly big it is."
Douglas Adams (1952–2001),
The Hitch Hiker's Guide to the Galaxy

TIME CHANGES

We think that time always passes at the same steady rate. We believe that a second is always a second, wherever we are or whatever we're doing. However, about 100 years ago, a scientist called Albert Einstein realized something amazing: how fast time passes depends on how fast the clock measuring time is moving.

Albert Einstein
(1879–1955)

Fast or slow?

Scientists tested Einstein's ideas. They took two accurate atomic clocks, both reading the same time, and put one on a plane. The plane flew round the Earth at high speed, and when it returned, the clock on board was a second or so behind the one on the ground. This is a tiny difference but it still proves that Einstein was right: the faster you go, the slower time passes.

Time travel?

Imagine you travelled for five years on a spaceship moving almost at the speed of light. You would be five years older on your return – but, on Earth, 36 years would have passed. You would return to the future!

You're my twin brother, but now you're 31 years older than me!

"There was a young lady named Bright,
Whose speed was far faster than light;
She set out one day
In a relative way
And returned on the previous night."
Arthur Buller (1874–1944), British scientist

TIME TRAVEL

In films like *Back to the Future* characters from the future meet people from the past!

Time travel is an exciting idea that has inspired many writers and film-makers. In time travel adventures, such as *Back to the Future* and *Doctor Who*, the characters don't just travel somewhere else, they also travel some*when* else. What sorts of things might happen if we could really travel to the future or back to the past? Here are a couple of possible situations.

A cancer cure! If I can take this back to the present, millions of lives will be saved!

Situation 1: A cure from the future?

If you could travel into the future, you could find the cure for diseases such as cancer. Would you be able to bring these cures 'back' and help the human race today?

Situation 2: Money from the past?

If you could travel back in time, you could make use of things you already know. For example, you could be the one to discover oil and become a millionaire. Would you still be rich on your return to the present?

This is going to make me rich in the future!

Don't get too excited: today's spaceships move much too slowly to make time travel a reality. However, who knows what new **technology** will bring? Only time will tell!

"There is no future in spending the present worrying about the past."
Anon.

GLOSSARY

atom the smallest piece of something

axis an imaginary line that runs through the centre of a planet. Each planet spins around its axis

conspicuous able to be seen clearly

galaxy a huge collection of stars

hemisphere each half of the Earth, usually divided by the equator and called the northern hemisphere and southern hemisphere

interval a period of time between two things

longitude any of the imaginary circles that pass around the Earth through both poles

orbit the path taken by one object around another – for example, the Earth around the Sun

pendulum a swinging wooden or metal rod with a weight on its lower end. It is used in some clocks to make them tick at the correct rate

quartz a crystal-like mineral found inside rocks. It can be made to vibrate and is used in clocks to make them tick at the right rate

species a group of animals or plants that are very similar

technology using scientific knowledge to produce useful things

time zone a part of the Earth with its own set time

vibration a rapid, back-and-forth movement

INDEX